GRAND HEART
Seasons: Devotions Through the Eyes of a Poet

GRAND HEART
Seasons: Devotions Through the Eyes of a Poet

Poems by **Gayle A. Carlson**
Watercolors by **Gwenna Merriman**

Just Dust Publishers
PO Box 19243
Portland OR 97280
JustDustPublishers.com

© 2015 by Just Dust Publishers
All rights reserved. Published 2015
No part of this book, neither text nor images, may be reproduced in any manner without permission from the publisher.
To obtain consent, contact: office@JustDustPublishers.com
Printed in the United States of America
First hardbound edition, 2015
ISBN: 978-0-9908635-5-7

Scripture quotations marked (NASB) taken from:
The New American Standard Bible, © 1995
by The Lockman Foundation Used by permission.

Scripture quotations marked (NLT) are taken from:
The Holy Bible, New Living Translation, © 2013 by Tyndale House Foundation Used by permission of Tyndale House Publishers, Inc. Carol Stream, Illinois 60188 All rights reserved.

Scripture quotations marked (AMP) are taken from:
The Amplified Bible, © 1987
by The Lockman Foundation Used by permission.

Scripture quotations marked (ESV®) are taken from:
The Holy Bible, English Standard Version®, copyright © 2001 by Crossway, a publishing ministry of Good News Publishers.
Used by permission. All rights reserved.

Scripture quotations marked (NIV) are taken from:
THE HOLY BIBLE, NEW INTERNATIONAL VERSION® NIV®
Copyright © 1973, 1978, 1984 by International Bible Society®
Used by permission. All rights reserved worldwide.

Scripture quotations marked (Phillips) are taken from:
The New Testament in Modern English, copyright □ 1958, 1959, 1960 J.B. Phillips and 1947, 1952, 1955, 1957 The Macmillian Company, New York. Used by permission. All rights reserved.

Cover and Interior Art: Gwenna Merriman
Cover and Interior Layout: Luke Carlson

In memory of Mother
who was equally accomplished in poetry and art,
and who shared her gifts with her two daughters.

Table of Contents

Preface 9

SPRING 11
Love Redefined 12
Diamonds 15
Spectrum of Seven 16
Do You Have an Israel? 19
Sea Gender Part 1 20
Sea Gender Part 2 23
Dormant Seed 24–25
Cross 26
Wait Three Days 29

SUMMER 31
Pastor 32
Fishing 35
Terrible Love 36
Unrelenting Gratefulness 39
Lovelife 40
While We Walked Together Home 43
Christian Thanksgiving 44
Progression 47

AUTUMN 49
Flecks of Gold 50
Condescensions 53
Ocean Waves 54
Prayer 57
How Long? 58
Intercession 61
Stepping Down 62–63

WINTER 65
Sunday Papers 66
Emotional Sea 68–71
Living Lie 73
The Rose 75
The Pearly Gates 76–77
Sunday Mourning 79
Last Right 80
Grand Heart 82–85

Acknowledgments 86

Preface

Poetry is a work of inspiration. Inspiration is divinely influenced insight, and therefore, a gift. The sudden intuition of a poem can be found anywhere and everywhere because that is where God is.

As art, the purpose of poetry is the arousal of emotion. As a Christian poet, my goal is the stimulation of beneficial emotion—the appreciation of God in His creation, a renewed love for His Word, the discovery of His daily mercies and the joyful acceptance of trial and struggle as the adhesive that holds us close to Him.

Poetry is as original as its writer. God blesses us with uniqueness and delights to see how we will channel Him to others, just as though we deliver a distinct bouquet—a fresh, inventive, and personally uplifting fragrance.

Word economy is the framework of a poem. The blank page is a canvas. Carefully chosen language is the colorful pigment. The structural appearance of poetry—its layout and shape—is critically important. My hope is that it draws, directs and rewards the eye as effectively as the viewing of a rich painting.

Most importantly, the reader's imagination is the catalyst that makes poetry worthwhile. Without an appreciative audience, poetry is vanity.

Thank you, dear reader, for ensuring my poems are not created in vain.

Spring

What better celebration of spring is there than to meditate on the vibrant life contained in God's gracious gifts? He has lavished His love upon us, saving us from ourselves and death. His light has opened the eyes of our understanding and we see the world in a colorful new perspective. He transforms us from the ordinary into the exceptional; He creates new life at every turn. The greatest gift, His Son, Jesus Christ—the agent through which He expresses all His nature—is humbly given to death, that we might be surprised, overjoyed, and forever blessed by His resurrection, as He springs up anew within us.

"How priceless is your unfailing love! Both high and low among men find refuge in the shadow of your wings."

Psalm 36:7 (NIV)

"How great is the love the Father has lavished on us, that we should be called children of God!"

1 John 3:1a (NIV)

"…we try to persuade men…For Christ's love compels us…"

2 Corinthians 5:11b & 14a (NIV)

Love Redefined

Vital gift—
violent, tragic Cross,
splitting apart Goodness
to repair evil.
We cry "mystery!"
Our dwarfed ideals
hold no candle
to this terrifying lightning.
What crazy Love
that suicidally ventures,
reclaiming those
ever bent to turn!
What driving,
pursuing obsession
that follows its way,
all the way,
to Hell and back
for me!

Necessary gift—
to review this awful Cross:
retelling sacrifice
to retrieve sinners.
We must cry "salvation!"
against the world's ideals
and hold a candle
to the murky darkness.
With whole devotion
we ought to wildly venture:
loving those unlovely,
who've bent and turned.
Drive on,
pursuing obsession,
that follows God's Way,
all the way,
to hell and back
for them!

Christ's dying love rescues us. His love through us can rescue others.

> "Therefore, if anyone is in Christ, he is a new creation.
> The old has passed away; behold, the new has come."
>
> 2 Corinthians 5:17 (ESV)

Diamonds

Coal deep,
below, below.
Pressed, stressed,
buried low.
Process aged,
old, cold.
Unseen, unknown—
long untold.

    Soul down,
    asleep, asleep.
    Drugged, mugged,
    hidden deep.
    Ageless Lord,
    wake, shake.
    Quicken, liven—
    sinew break.

        Coal change,
        arise, arise.
        Bright white,
        dazzle eyes.
        Ancient Way,
        new, true.
        Diamonds found—
        me and you.

Christ brings nothing less than total transformation.

> "...Christ will be revealed from heaven by the blessed and only almighty God,
> the King of all kings and Lord of all lords. He alone can never die,
> and he lives in light so brilliant that no human can approach him.
> No human eye has ever seen him, nor ever will.
> All honor and power to him forever! Amen."
>
> 1 Timothy 6:15b & 16 (NLT)

Spectrum of Seven

Our Maker,
dwelling in unapproachable Light,
opens Himself to us,
knowing we cannot survive
    His pure whiteness.

And so,
kindly and wisely,
He diffuses Himself
through Christ our Savior,
the prism of His wisdom,
into rainbow-covenant colors:
    The Son's red-death sacrifice;
      blood of promise that whitens our sins.
    The Judge's rust-orange scepter;
      iron Sovereignty of absolute rule.
    The Messiah's golden Glory;
      yellow-gold Divinity crowned with power.
    The Vine's green fruitfulness;
      verdant blessings of life that grows.
    The Morning Star's blue heavens;
      righteous perfection forever, sky high.
    The Great High Priest's indigo clothing;
      His cover that darkens with rich atonement.
And the King's violet robe;
      The royal purple our Majesty deserves.

God is Light faceted into every color.

> "I do not want you to be ignorant of this mystery, brothers, so that you may not be conceited: Israel has experienced a hardening in part until the full number of the Gentiles has come in. And so all Israel will be saved, as it is written: 'The deliverer will come from Zion; he will turn godlessness away from Jacob. And this is my covenant with them when I take away their sins.'"
>
> Romans 11:25–27 (NIV)

Do You Have an Israel?

Do you have an "Israel,"
a person who is "blind?"
A someone who refuses God,
who does not know Christ's mind?

Do you have an "Israel,"
a "first love" turned untrue?
A someone who "lip-serves" the Lord,
whose goals are not with you?

Do you have an "Israel,"
a soul backslidden far,
who murmurs and complains 'gainst God,
whose life the cross does mar?

Do you have an "Israel,"
like Christ, for whom you mourn?
He wished that He could gather them
close to Him—newly born.

Do you have an "Israel,"
like Paul, for whom you'd die?
If that one could but see the light—
be lifted up on high!

If you have an "Israel,"
be comforted, my friend:
our God Almighty understands
and works a happy end.

For one day darkened Israel
will shine with light so bright—
their day will come—a special one—
no longer lost in night.

All of time has been a plan,
with Israel at the heart;
is it not the same for you?
Keep praying—do your part.

Then watch, and wait to see unfold
God's Mighty Saving Hand;
both Israel and your Lost One—
they will possess the Land!

Lost loved ones? God knows all about it!

> *"God called the dry ground 'land,' and the gathered waters he called 'seas.'
> And God saw that it was good."*
>
> Genesis 1:10 (NIV)

Sea Gender—Part 1

Mother cliffs
stand at shore,
secure, reliable, protective.
Manly waves advance
      upon them.
Coves are
warm wombs,
welcoming the power, life and strength
      of the sea;
yet the waters
assail mercilessly—
often grinding
rock to powder.
The push and aggression
does not mock rock though;
sea and shore
      coexist. Where they touch, life thrives.
Man must move—restlessly conquering.
Woman remains seated—serenely planted.

Sea Gender—Part 2

The cyclical sea,
like woman,
heaves with emotion,
throwing herself
upon the
bastion of strong man—
the solid tower rocks.
Her mood tides
rise and wane,
       yet he,
unmoved,
holds the line of her flow.
He is her sheltering fortress.
But she influences continually
       against his domination,
changing him sometimes
to sand.
She, the water, fluidly cold or warm.
He, the stone, firm and monumental.

Masculine and feminine: aren't both contained in the nature of God?

*"I planted the seed in your hearts, and Apollos watered it,
but it was God who made it grow."*

1 Corinthians 3:6 (NLT)

Dormant Seed

The Scott's super grass seed that cost me a ton
was blue and nutritious and moist all in one.
I laid it on top of rich topsoil to boot.
I scattered it thickly; I said, "More is good!"

    God's teachings, so precious, so priceless 'tis true,
    are red with Christ's blood to transform me and you.
    I laid them all out with the curl of my tongue—
    my speech overbearing—was trouble begun?

The grass seed instructions in tiny display
gave temperature rules: today was okay!
And six days 'til sprouts! I was happy indeed!
But twelve cold days later, no grass, woe is me!

    The sermon receivers, both wincing and hurt,
    were clearly offended by what I did blurt.
    'Twas not a good day, and I was not glad.
    As many days passed—no response—things looked bad!

Then I, largely doubtful, neglected the lawn—
gave only brief sprinklings of water anon.
On day twenty-one, small weak shoots! Hallelu!
Now diligent care with more hope did ensue.

    I backed off completely—left hearers alone;
    free will, after all, is a gift we all own.
    But several weeks later there came a faint knock:
    just thought they'd stop by—yes, they wanted to talk!

Now daily I'm checking the status of grass;
the rain and the sun are increasing its mass.
The shoots are now blades and they've thickened—do tell!
I smile and I'm joyed—this is going quite well!

    Now daily the prayers for God's seed to conceive
    are rising for those who have heard and believed.
    The giving of time, and His love which is true,
    are reaping results! I rejoice! God's not through!

At last all the patches of grass could be mown.
The seeds I had thrown had matured, fully grown.
They'd sprung up, and finally, (good deal!), blended in!
My costly investment has paid off! I win!

    Just now I'm observing the Lord giving grace
    to those I had hammered back then, face to face.
    In spite of me, Father, they've sprouted some green!
    It's all due to You, Lord, and Your Hand unseen!

The good seed of God's Word prospers in His time.

"For the word of the cross is folly to those who are perishing, but to us who are being saved it is the power of God."

1 Corinthians 1:18 (ESV)

Cross

Horizontal relationships
    us to us
    flat across the dusty earth
    imitation of dedication
    illusively together
    virtually apart

Vertical relationship
    God to us
    Heaven's path straight down to earth
    recreation of devotion
    forever together
    never apart

Cross relationship
    God with us
    Heav'n descends to join the earth
    collision in crucifixion
    momentarily dead
    eternally alive

The cross is God's essential idea.

28

"He was buried, and he was raised from the dead on the third day, just as the Scriptures said."

1 Corinthians 15:4 (NLT)

Wait Three Days

Write a poem.
      Wait three days.
Marinate the mood.
Oven-heat it
to bake off the raw edges.

Window shop.
      Wait three days.
Improve impulses
into disciplined decisions
'til need conquers want.

Form your argument.
      Wait three days.
Subside the tide.
Ebb the flow to reveal
other life considerations.

Kill the Master.
      Wait three days.
Silent Sovereignty
revives stolen life,
raising Him and our hope.

A little time can make a big difference.

Summer

Summertime wraps us in its heat. Our lives flourish. We prosper and increase, reaching out warmly to one another. Gratitude begins to fill every moment as we plumb the depths of what God's love is really all about. Our relationships take on new meaning under the greenhouse effect of forgiveness and thanksgiving. We learn more readily from those who lead us, becoming eternally grateful for how God uses those He has placed around us. Best of all, we rejoice in our growth in Christ as we realize the amazing scope of His ongoing acceptance of us, and the deepening intimacy we have with God.

> *"Obey your spiritual leaders, and do what they say.*
> *Their work is to watch over your souls, and they are accountable to God."*
>
> Hebrews 13:17a (NLT)

Pastor

You make me face God,
   not layering Him
   between the pages of Scripture only,
   not channeling Him
   through yourself or others only,
   not cornering Him
   into ideas or creeds alone,
      though all of these help me.
You help me help myself to Him
      alone Who is,
   blessedly ineffable,
   delightfully mysterious,
   ever loftier than our growing understandings,
   Creator over creature forever.

You make me face Him,
   teaching with effortless de-emphasis
   all those human how-to's,
   reaching my spirit at its heart
   with all your heart,
   living honestly your own unknowns
   all wide open to me,
      which aims me ever to Him.

You make me face The LORD.

The best spiritual leaders never come between you and God.

33

"A friend is always loyal, and a brother is born to help in time of need."
Proverbs 17:17 (NLT)

Fishing

Stretch out,
far-flung heart,
with taut line
and tacit lure.

Hungry again
I seek to catch
friendship's flesh—
the tenuous yet companionable heartbeat
of another's life.

Fly out,
reeling hope.
My net lies slack.
Has it ever slumped roomier
at my anxious feet?

Nevertheless
I smile assuredly—
the season is new
the water, clear,

And there are
many, many friends
in the sea.

Friendship is never far away: it's as near as my kindness to another.

"...the LORD thy God is among you, a mighty God and terrible."
Deuteronomy 7:21b (KJV)

Terrible Love

I quake in terror
of Your Love,
oh Lord.
It is
too much,
the way You
killed Yourself
for me.
I deserved
    the reprimand,
    the punishment,
    the death-blow.
But You
twisted back
upon Yourself
those mockings,
that whip,
My Cross.
    And viewing the Calvary hill
    I shake in fear of You!
    Who are You,
    Alien Lover?
    From what far realm
    have You flown to rescue me?
    Why invade
    this dense,
    and blind,
    and self-filled
    world?
    I quake in terror
    of Your Love,
    oh Lord.

No one ever gave to another as much as God has given to us.

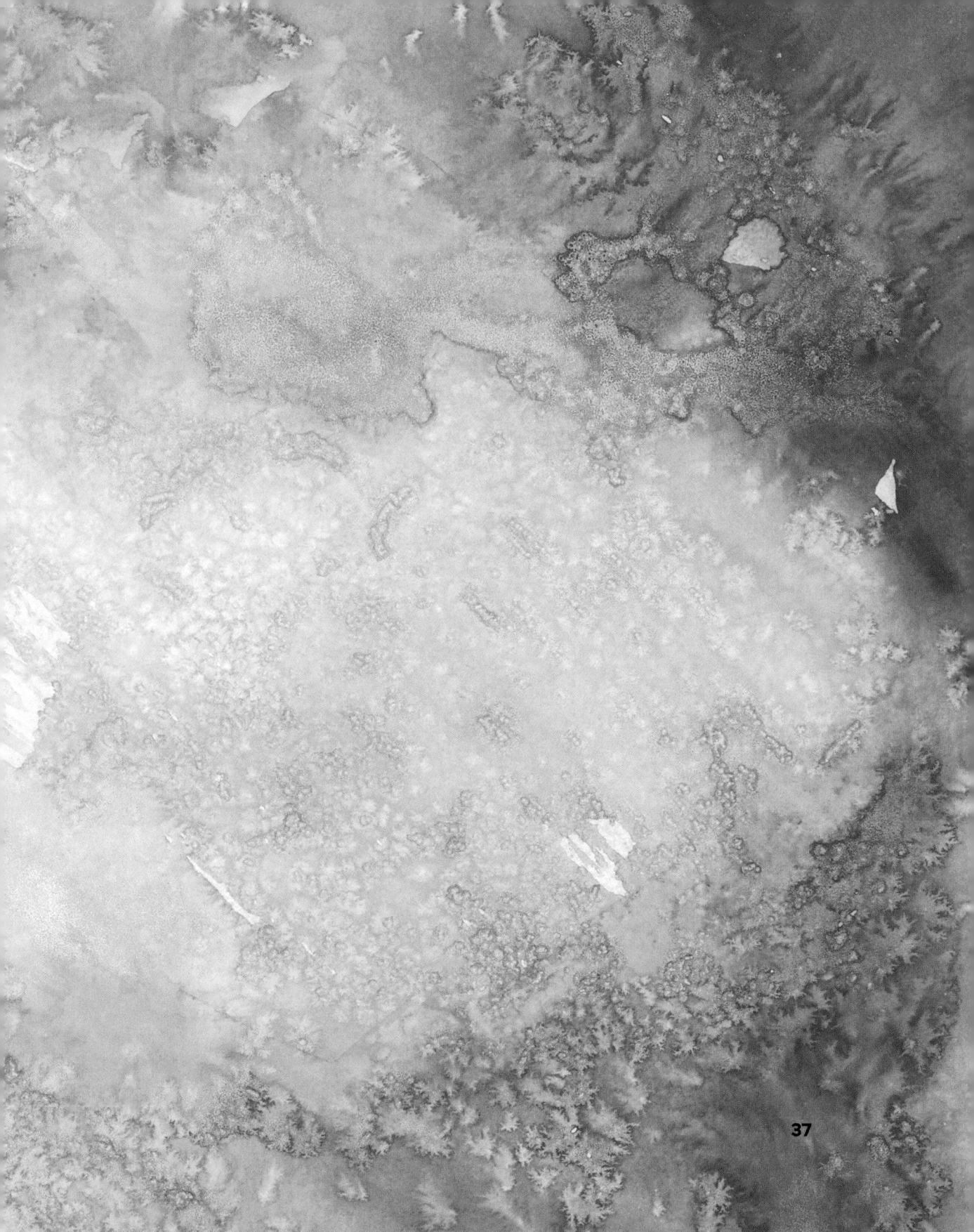

"But seek first the kingdom of God and his righteousness, and all these things will be added to you."

Matthew 6:33 (ESV)

Unrelenting Gratefulness

God's generous green-life giving
occasions a pearly
spirit-juice ooze,
an unrelenting gratefulness.

Its flow grows,
rolls obligingly ocher-orange,
then pours appreciatively red-rouge,
drenching neutral days.

Our wide bright smiles
contentedly discern Him
in every lively quarter.

Now opalescent, we
golden-glow with
gladness,
seeing ever and again
God's generous green-life giving.

An "attitude of gratitude" changes everything.

> *"Whoever believes in me, as the Scripture has said,*
> *'Out of his heart will flow rivers of living water.'"*
>
> John 10:11 (ESV)

Lovelife

Thank You, Lord
that our entrance
into the universe of Your Love-giving
is invigorated with possibilities.
There is no limit to
the adventurous challenges
of walking
where You walked.
The potential discoveries
are as electrifying as
new worlds,
stars,
galaxies.
As much of ourselves as we yield to You,
You give back
in magnification
by channeling Your Life
in,
through,
out.
We are gushing waterways,
pleasured abundantly
by the sweet swell of Your Lovelife in us
flowing to the thirsty.

Love, like water, is fully alive when flowing.

"I am the good shepherd. The good shepherd lays down his life for the sheep."

John 10:11 (ESV)

While We Walked Together Home

I just assumed
because I'd slipped so stupidly,
fallen so wildly,
that He'd be far away.
Wouldn't my behavior push Him off?
But no.
It was then I really learned
He was My Shepherd,
searching o'er the roughest rocks
for His one wayward rebel.
He had prepared
His special, private, kinder words,
more tender, gentler strokes just then
for me.
He gave them to me
while we walked together home.

Christ's forgiving love always surprises me.

"Give thanks in all circumstances; for this is the will of God in Christ Jesus for you."
1 Thessalonians 5:18 (ESV)

Christian Thanksgiving

Be thankful for gain;
God is behind all prosperity.
    Be thankful for loss;
    in it we find we cannot lose God.
Be thankful for health;
God is sustaining your body.
    Be thankful for pain;
    it can lead to pleasure in God.
Be thankful for blessings;
God is the source of all good gifts.
    Be thankful for trouble;
    it can turn us toward God.
Be thankful for supply;
God is meeting all needs.
    Be thankful for want;
    there is none with God.
Be thankful for sudden joys;
God lifts our hearts to Him.
    Be thankful to wait;
    it creates focus on God.
Be thankful for laughter;
God thrills to hear us rejoice.
    Be thankful for sorrow;
    God's true joy overcomes.
Be thankful for life;
God is good to give it.
    Be thankful for death;
    God's eternal life conquers death.

Gratefulness in all situations brings complete peace.

"My beloved is mine, and I am his…"

Song of Solomon 2:16 (NASB)

Progression

God!
    Love above
    Radiate
    Own, atone
    Consecrate
        Kill my will
        Subjugate
        King of kings
        Dominate
            Slake my ache
            Satiate
            Enter my center
            Penetrate
                Cover me, Lover
                Consummate.

"Jesus, Lover of my soul, let me to thy bosom fly."—Charles Wesley

48

Autumn

The cooling breezes of fall often bring some challenges our way. We may feel the pressure of innumerable difficulties, but God permits these downward pushes, exposing priceless lessons at every turn. Our dialogue with God may find us crying out like small children as God works to transform impatience into endurance, pride into humility and selfishness into prayerful concern for others around us. The golden hues of fruitful aging in our lives are His blessings reaching maturity in us as we value the decreasing of self and the increase of His attributes and constancy.

"For God knew his people in advance, and he chose them to become like his Son, so that his Son would be the firstborn among many brothers and sisters."
Romans 8:29 (NLT)

Flecks of Gold

How many the flecks of gold,
    dashes of Divinity,
mingling in the sand!
I only see them though
when waves
stretch the sands out flat
and only when the sun
is high and bright.

How many the lives of gold,
    displays of Divinity,
mingling in the world!
I only see them though
when trials
stretch their lives out flat
and only when their Son
is High and Bright.

We are "Christians": "little Christs."

> "…and whoever would be first among you must be slave of all. For even the Son of Man came not to be served but to serve, and to give his life as a ransom for many."
>
> Mark 10:44–45 (ESV)

Condescensions

Authoritative Godhead
    dips down to
        infancy and childhood—
            (to save all mankind.)
Transfigured Messiah
    treks down into
        devil-filled valley—
            (to aid the demoniac.)
Resurrection Jublilance
    winds down to
        breakfast of fish—
            (to encourage the disciples.)
Amazing Ascension
    fades away into
        daily discipling duties—
            (to reach all the lost.)
Ecstasy of Blood-washing
    drains down to
        forgiveness of others—
            (to act out our faith.)

Most often the quickest way up is down.

*"Talk no more so very proudly, let not arrogance come from your mouth;
for the Lord is a God of knowledge, and by him actions are weighed."*

1 Samuel 2:3 (ESV)

Ocean Waves

Ocean waves
fingerprint their way
across the sand paper—
ridge overlaying ridge.
Yet their touches
erase
every other mark inscribed,
leaving only
their powerfully level, cooling identity.
    None of my
    footprints
    remain.
    Was I ever here?
Perhaps this is
what comforts me most:
losing the
imprint of me amidst
Ocean waves.

It is good to want God to increase and self to decrease.

"Don't worry over anything whatever; tell God every detail of your needs in earnest and thankful prayer, and the peace of God, which transcends human understanding, will keep constant guard over your hearts and minds as they rest in Christ Jesus."
— Philippians 4:6–7 (PHILLIPS)

Prayer

Cease spinning;
back to Center.
Catch complaints
to sing a praise.
Stand reasoning
in faith's corner.
Set impulses
beneath His gaze.

And sit down
        long enough
to let go.

Prayer changes the ones who pray: it teaches them to relinquish things.

> *"How long, O LORD? Will you forget me forever?*
> *How long will you hide your face from me?"*
>
> Psalm 13:1b (ESV)
>
> *"O LORD, how long shall I cry for help, and you will not hear?*
> *Or cry to you 'Violence!' and you will not save?"*
>
> Habakkuk 1:5 (ESV)

How Long?

"How long?" The querulous, agonized words
 arise in my suffering heart.
 How long to process pain awaiting
 consummate calm with relief?
"How long?" I dread will lag unto death,
 only Heaven my distant ease,
 my Father's full face my only consoling,
 escape, my lone motto and creed.

"How long?" The script the Father has written
 still wraps round my life like a shroud.
 Yet lovingly I know He lays it;
 grace glistens in every thread.
 I've known there's a treasure well-hidden
 because of His smile and care.
"How long?" seems transcendent o'er earth, over time,
 o'er me as an armored defense.

"How long?" I now hear Him whisper to me,
"how long could you lay on my breast?
 How long can you but bask in my breath,
 commune, enjoy my embrace?
 How long could we walk under the clouds,
 your hand in My long-wounded one?
 How long companion in heartbroken nearness?
 I AM Heaven—I'll not forsake."

Then down the pathway another "How long?"
 drifts like a sweet fragrance soothing,
"How long will Eternity's gladness
 endure then—sorrow all gone?
 How long's everlasting? Forever?
 How long with sin banished and burned?"
"How long?" has become most precious in language,
 since Christ, Author, Finisher reigns!

Our impatience is neutralized by God's eternality.

> "Pray at all times—on every occasion, in every season—in the Spirit, with all manner of prayer and entreaty. To that end keep alert and watch with strong purpose and perseverance, interceding on behalf of all the saints (God's consecrated people)."
>
> Ephesians 6:18 (AMP)

Intercession

I prayed for you today.
I can only pray
      what is truth to me.
I recall the
blessed, hurtful leanings/weanings
      that bent me to His arms.
I want you bent there, too,
      sent there, too,
to learn the precious pain
of a cut umbilical dependency on earth.

To pray real love is hard.
I must only pray
      what you really need.
I refuse the
silken, luxury easings/pleasings
      that build an idol's form.
I want you burning them,
      spurning them,
to find the mysterious joy
of treasure buried far away in Heaven.

Prayer for others is our most real labor of love.

*"Let this same attitude and purpose and humble mind be in you which was in Christ Jesus—
let Him be your example in humility—Who, although being essentially one with God
and in the form of God possessing the fullness of the attributes which make God God,
did not think this equality with God was a thing to be eagerly grasped or retained;
but stripped Himself of all privileges and rightful dignity so as to assume the guise of a
servant (slave), in that He became like men and was born a human being. And after
He had appeared in human form He abased and humbled Himself still further and carried
His obedience to the extreme of death, even the death of the cross! Therefore because
He stooped so low, God has highly exalted Him and has freely bestowed on Him the name
that is above every name, that at the name of Jesus every knee must bow,
in heaven and on earth and under the earth, and every tongue frankly and openly
confess and acknowledge that Jesus Christ is Lord, to the glory of God the Father."*

Philippians 2:5–11 (AMP)

Stepping Down

He was elected to step down:
awakening into flesh,
smelling His created cattle,
the Father fitting Omnipresence
into fetal skin.
      A baby step.

He chose to step down:
growing within Jewry,
the simple life, anonymity,
watering down Kingly Divinity
into grass roots servanthood.
      A people step.

He preferred to step down:
moving into dissension,
opposing traditional ways,
stripping, rattling men's false truth
with Immanuel language.
      A God step.

He agreed to a fateful step down:
undeservedly deep into ignominious death,
permitting Roman hands
to capture and nail down
the Indefinable Jehovah.
      The devil's step.

Satan took Him down yet again:
dragging God into Hell,
doubtlessly to The Pit's absolute bottom,
all our sins pressing Him there,
a power play on Omnipotence.
      Evil's final step.

      Each downward step,
      each humbling of self,
      is a long-term deposit
      in Heaven's vaults.

For now is Christ raised:
returning Home to Glory,
leading bright children behind Him,
we, God's people, elevated, exalted,
and He to the highest point.
      The fantastic up-fruit
      of all our down-steps.

"God will exalt those who have humbled themselves."

Winter

Signs of life seem to disappear during the cold of winter. In this spiritual season the world, the flesh, and the devil may take the upper hand. We may cave into our carnality or end up cooperating with the world too much. At these times God may send His quickest and most effective tools of pain and suffering to expose our sin and failure and to strip away the film that lies over our soul's eyes. Suddenly we discern the beauty of this frigid time of year: an unsurpassed elegance not to be found at any other time. We come to comprehend more deeply the mystery of Christ's death and anguish.

"Open my eyes, that I may behold wondrous things out of your law."
Psalm 119:18 (ESV)

Sunday Papers

Conspicuous front-porch pages
drop and shock on the
threshold of days.
Though inviting to covet
with bright-slick allure,
these banners of the bed
are drowsy-scanned—
eyes
sewn together
with sleep.

Unobtrusive shelf-gracing volume
tucked and kept in the
background of lives.
Since plainly mysterious,
with deep-sought pleasure,
this Divine diary
must be Spirit-read—
hearts
thrown open
with prayer.

We are what we read.

67

"Have you journeyed to the springs of the sea or walked in the recesses of the deep?"
Job 38:16 (NIV)

"There is the sea, vast and spacious, teeming with creatures beyond number—living things both large and small."
Psalm 104:25 (NIV)

Emotional Sea

Have you seen the emotional sea?
    Powered water
    surges the shoreline,
    overwhelming humanity's earthy edge.
    Rocks of reason reduce
    to under wave, underfoot
        bits of grit.
Passionate, majestic sea of emotion!
    Artists dwell there.
    The Lonely find drowning grounds
        for their pain
    in its deafening demonstrations.
        Crashing, crushing,
            the whole world must listen.
            Every eye must look.
Curled water
drives froth as proof,
pulverizing even
my simple life.
        Waves stand erect like our proud heads
then capitulate complainingly,
flattening our spirits
into low troughs
and far-reaching floods.
        The tears fall everywhere.
And sadly,
at lowest tide,
the ocean often offers up voiceless victims,
    displaying death
        on its doorstep.

Have you looked under the emotional sea?
    Another world,
    secretive, deeply silent,
    abundant with life
    never realized on the surface.
    Color cacophonies coexist
    in unsullied balance.
        A greater power rules.
Treasured, exquisite undersea realm!
    The spiritual dwell there.
    Seekers acquire capsuled breath
        to navigate their course.
        Quietly, invisibly,
            the whole world cannot watch.
            Only a sparse handful sees.
    Calmed water
    surrounds all in peace,
    empowering even
    my simple life.
        Fish schools flick electrically like charged
    messengers scattering from view,
    whetting our minds
    to know their Maker
    and our Designer.
        His joy triumphs everywhere.
    And gladly,
    at fullest Day,
    the deep daily delivers plentiful provision,
        laying life
        at our disposal.

Our emotions cry for attention; but time with God is a better investment.

*"You hate my instruction and cast my words behind you…
You use your mouth for evil and harness your tongue to deceit."*

Psalm 50:17 & 19 (NIV)

Living Lie

Eat the lie.
Wash the crooked down
with make-believe.
Swallow deceptions whole.
Worldlings dare you:
copy them
without choking.
You'll get used to it;
addicted, more like.
Soon the Rock's honey
cannot be stomached,
neither the salt of the earth,
and too late
the discovery:
you are what you eat.

A committed love for God's Word is completely indispensable.

> *"...remembering the words the Lord Jesus himself said:*
> *'It is more blessed to give than to receive.'"*
>
> Acts 20:35b (NIV)

The Rose

I wonder
at the rose.
Extravagant with her petals,
casting down her beauty,
bleeding out exotic fragrance,
generously giving away life
in dying/flying colors
while so few saw.

How unlike us
who grasp and pull to self,
exalting beauty in every mirror,
closely clutching our importance
with gnawing greed,
dying daily in dark/stark blackness
while the whole world watches,
and wonders.

Lord, help me to be as gracious and generous as a rose!

"And the twelve gates were twelve pearls; each one of the gates was a single pearl…"
Revelation 21:21a (NASB)

The Pearly Gates

Twelve splendid entryways
the Heav'nly City touts;
"Twelve gates of single pearls!"
the C'lestial angel shouts.

I looked, and wondered,
why of pearl?
What means this precious stone?
A whisper answered,
"Take a look
At God's deep myst'ries shown:

Pearls come from suffering,
from grit within the shell.
Pearl is the conqueror;
its gloss the pain to quell."

I view and see that
in we come,
through tribulations swirled.
Yet Jesus told us,
"Have good cheer:
I've overcome the world."

Twelve shining gates of white
has New Jerusalem;
twelve testified His truth
near old Jerusalem.

The tested twelve,
were tried and killed
much like their King and Guide.
Through pain their beauty
grows unseen;
like pearls in oysters hide.

Twelve wondrous entrances
around our Home abide.
Twelve doors as ways to come
to reach Our Lord inside.

Through suffering and
pain on earth
we find our only way;
But then we'll own a
sweeter joy
that ne'er will slip away.

Without suffering there would be no beautiful pearls.

"Those who live in the shelter of the Most High will find rest in the shadow of the Almighty. This I declare about the LORD: He alone is my refuge, my place of safety; he is my God, and I trust him."

Psalm 91:1-2 (NLT)

Sunday Mourning

Here come all the hurting souls:
weepers washing down the aisles.
Wills straining up their Calvarys,
pressing forward to this altar.
Kneeling under watersheds of sanctuary,
    crying.
Bowing beneath Sovereignty of Godhead,
    choosing.
Following hard after perfection of faith,
    failing.
They seek another City.
Standing up among the seated,
bringing their baggage with them,
loaded, longing to unload.
Here come all the hurting souls.

"God whispers to us in our pleasures, speaks in our consciences, but shouts in our pains." —C.S. Lewis

> "Opponents must be gently instructed, in the hope that God will grant them repentance leading them to a knowledge of the truth, and that they will come to their senses and escape from the trap of the devil, who has taken them captive to do his will."
>
> 2 Timothy 2:25 & 26 (NIV)

Last Right

They cast
their sour trash remains
on the beloved breast
of God's sweet earth.
    We smell
    the hating
    of His presence.

    They charge,
    like red-angry bulls,
    through their God-bestowed,
    mercy-riddled lives.
        We see
        the ignoring
        of His presence.

    They die,
    upholding the persistent
    refusing of Christ,
    as their God-given,
    and last, right.
        We mourn
        the rejecting
        of His presence.

Nothing is more tragic than free will exercised against God.

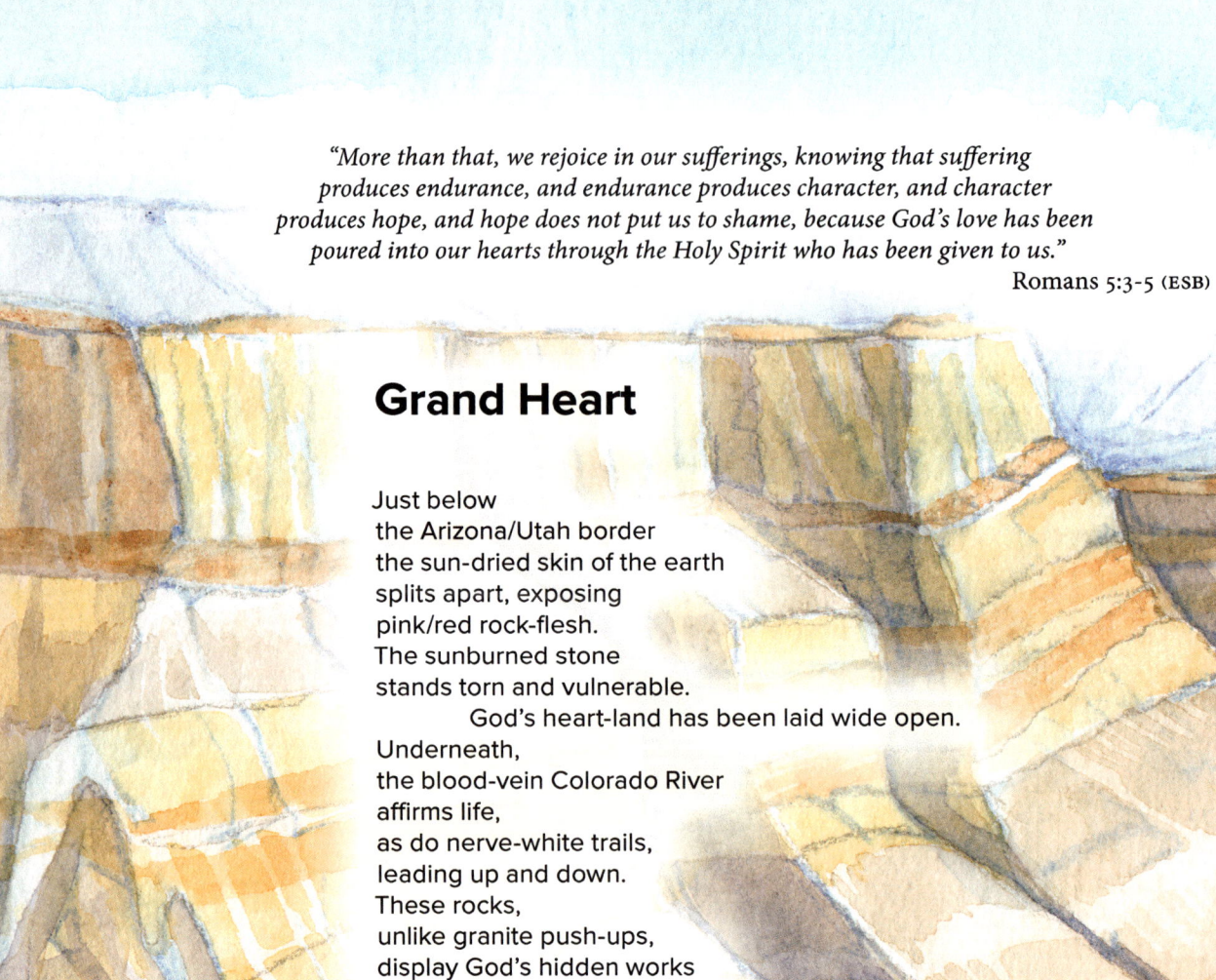

> *"More than that, we rejoice in our sufferings, knowing that suffering produces endurance, and endurance produces character, and character produces hope, and hope does not put us to shame, because God's love has been poured into our hearts through the Holy Spirit who has been given to us."*
>
> Romans 5:3-5 (ESB)

Grand Heart

Just below
the Arizona/Utah border
the sun-dried skin of the earth
splits apart, exposing
pink/red rock-flesh.
The sunburned stone
stands torn and vulnerable.
    God's heart-land has been laid wide open.
Underneath,
the blood-vein Colorado River
affirms life,
as do nerve-white trails,
leading up and down.
These rocks,
unlike granite push-ups,
display God's hidden works
in stunning striations—
    foreordained plans,
    layered during
the laying down
    of the stored secrets of time;
    each of His Truths a different color,
    each of His Ways a unique creative pattern.

Both canyon and mountain
stand monumentally mute
speaking majesty.
To mountain, we look up;
yet here,
we gape down from life's rim,
into artwork seemingly born of pain,
somehow much more speechless.
    God draws us to this descending view,
    revealing again and anew,
    His Heart:
    out of suffering—
    an unparalleled
    Beauty.

Can our hearts also stand,
    pained and opened,
as silently,
as handsomely,
as enduringly?

**May God's love, perfected through pain, fill us and overflow to others—
the unparalleled beauty of His Grand Heart.**

Acknowledgments

I would like to thank many over the years who have encouraged me to "keep on writing." You are all vital friends. Sal Coxe Dobbs and Ann Applegarth, writing companions who critiqued my poems and gave precious advice. Annette Cone, without her nudges and encouragement this book would not exist. Shelley Houston and Dusti Johnson, God used you to bring this book to print. My dear sister, Gwenna Merriman, whose watercolors grace every page of the book—your art is amazing! My wonderful son, Dr. Luke Carlson, for laboring carefully to put art, writing, and scripture together into a beautiful layout.

And my Lord, Jesus Christ. He is the life in every poem.